a
and Your

T0407323

In a day of endless comparison, body image can be a painful and unrelenting struggle. We battle with dissatisfaction, shame, and self-doubt when the image in the mirror doesn't look like ideals on our screens. Julie Lowe has written a brief, accessible book for teens to help them navigate this challenge as they learn to find hope in their identity in Christ. Whether you are a teen, parent a teen, or serve with teens at your church, *Track: A Student's Guide to Body Image* will serve you well.

Brad Hambrick
Pastor of Counseling, The Summit Church,
Raleigh, North Carolina;
author, *Transformative Friendships*

TRACK
CHRISTIAN
LIFE

A STUDENT'S GUIDE TO
BODY IMAGE

JULIE
LOWE

SERIES EDITED BY
JOHN PERRITT

CHRISTIAN
FOCUS

rym

Unless otherwise stated, Scripture quotations are from *The Holy Bible, English Standard Version*, copyright © 2001 by Crossway Bibles, a publishing ministry of Good News Publishers. Used by permission. All rights reserved. ESV Text Edition: 2011.

Scripture quotations marked NIV are taken from the Holy Bible, New International Version®, NIV® Copyright ©1973, 1978, 1984, 2011 by Biblica, Inc.® Used by permission. All rights reserved worldwide.

Scripture quotations from the King James Version are marked with KJV.

Copyright © Julie Lowe 2024

paperback ISBN 978-1-5271-1004-5

ebook ISBN 978-1-5271-1206-3

10 9 8 7 6 5 4 3 2 1

First published in 2024
by
Christian Focus Publications Ltd,
Geanies House, Fearn,
Ross-shire, IV20 1TW, Great Britain
www.christianfocus.com

with

Reformed Youth Ministries,
1445 Rio Road East Suite 201D
Charlottesville, Virginia, 22911

Cover by MOOSE77

Printed and bound by Gutenberg, Malta

CONTENTS

Series Introduction

Christianity is a religion of words, because our God is a God of words. He created through words, calls Himself the Living Word, and wrote a book (filled with words) to communicate to His children. In light of this, pastors and parents should take great efforts to train the next generation to be readers. *Track* is a series designed to do exactly that.

Written for students, the *Track* series addresses a host of topics in three primary areas: Doctrine, Culture, and the Christian Life. *Track's* booklets are theologically rich, yet accessible. They seek to engage and challenge the student without dumbing things down.

One definition of a track reads: *a way that has been formed by someone else's footsteps.* The goal of the *Track* series is to point us to that 'someone else'—Jesus Christ. The One who forged a track to guide His followers. While we cannot follow this track perfectly, by His grace and Spirit He calls us to strive to stay on the path. It is our prayer that this series of books would help guide Christ's Church until He returns.

In His service,

John Perritt
RYM's Director of Resources
Series Editor

1. Our Battle with the Mirror

Katie is a nineteen-year-old college student who has struggled with body image issues since she was eleven years old.

It began while observing her mom and older sister talk about their displeasure with their weight. They would complain their thighs were too big or their nose was too small and discuss what they could do to make improvements. Often, mealtime conversations revolved around incessant dialogue about diet and nutrition, or how much they should restrict to maintain a "healthy" appearance.

As Katie developed, it became obvious there were all kinds of unwritten rules at home about what foods were acceptable and which were taboo. Good ideas of health and eating were intermingled with unhealthy ideals for weight, image and beauty. Katie found herself comparing her own pre-adolescent body to that of her thin, image-conscious older sister. She developed food rituals and rules, as well as unrealistic standards she forced upon herself.

As Katie entered middle and high school, the sea of comparison grew to include peers and social media. She noticed friends posting pictures of themselves in new outfits and semi-promiscuous poses on social media, getting tons of likes and positive comments. It was a constant prompt to evaluate her appearance accordingly. Katie found herself chasing standards and consistently trying to measure up to what public opinion held as ideal. She regularly felt inadequate.

In an attempt to fulfill the ideal appearance, she checked how she looked in the mirror regularly, exercised obsessively and teetered on the edge of anorexia. Katie became anxious attending social events, uncertain of how others viewed her, or desperate to get compliments. She spent hours surfing social media to see what people were wearing, what the newest beauty trends were and to make sure she was not missing out. She tried to keep up with developing her own online "image," becoming preoccupied with who was following her on social media. She would count how many "likes" she received from others and feel depressed when there was little response.

Katie explained to her counselor what she was experiencing: "I am constantly looking in the mirror. From when I am picking out my outfit, to when I am leaving school, just thinking about if I am walking weird. I feel like everyone I know is struggling with this. Maybe some more than others. Sometimes I need to remind myself that, and it gives me this feeling of reassurance. I am not the only one that's stressed about my outfit that day or how my hair looks. When I think about my friends that I love so much, it has nothing to do with how they look. We also notice fifty more flaws about ourselves than everyone else does.

We all are seeking some form of self-approval from others. I want to be seen as pretty, nice, funny, stylish and many other things in other people's eyes, but why someone likes you should be way beyond your looks. I will try to dress like other people to fit in, but I also find myself trying to wear different unique things to stand out and be seen. I just want to be seen, and to fit in. I want to be funny, but I don't want to speak out and embarrass myself, and it's all so confusing to me – why?"

Always worrying about how people perceive us can lead to being stressed and anxious, which can impact grades, mood, confidence and self-image. When you are trying to impress a certain person and it seems like it's not working, what do you do? Do you create a fake personality or change your looks just to fit in and get attention? What happens when your true self begins to show? Will they judge you? Will they still like you?

Unknowingly, Katie's struggle with the mirror had become her idol; it was the thing that ruled her. She was at times blind to how much she clung to the need to find value in her outward appearance. It seemed "normal" – what every girl (and guy) her age did, and it became the thing she worshiped. By the time Katie entered her freshman year of college she was both gripped by, and depressed over, her inability to measure up. She lost interest in spending time with friends because she could not enjoy them. They had become a measuring stick of her own successes or failures and this way of living was leading her to despair.

Perhaps you can sympathize with Katie; maybe you even see yourself in her. My guess is, to some degree or another, we each can identify with her struggle.

Although body image struggles have previously been thought to be a struggle primarily of women, that is no longer the case. Boys and men alike are falling victim to similar stereotypes and pressures in an image obsessed culture. Young boys who are bullied due to weight or appearance, teen boys who feel the pressure to look tough, build muscle and have a model build, men who must be polished, lean, muscular, attractive and desirable. There is an onslaught of messages facing young men and women alike, instructing them that their outward appearance defines them.

MAIN IDEA

We are all worshipers and can be tempted to find our worth in the wrong things.

REFLECTION QUESTIONS

- How are you similar to Katie? How do you see yourself in her story?
- What are things you may be strongly tempted to worship? Why?
- Can you think of ways it impacts your daily life?

2. Does Scripture Speak to This?

As Christians, the Scriptures are our ultimate authority on life. It is where we find an accurate picture of ourselves. If you read Katie's story closely, you will have noticed a few things:

- What those around her **said** and how they **lived** made a large impact on how Katie interpreted reality.
- Her friends and society at large began to **shape** her interpretations and values, and thus how she **viewed** herself.

God, being a good father, knows we are not in a position to make sense out of life left to ourselves. In the Garden of Eden, God did not leave Adam and Eve by themselves to make sense out of their environment. Humanity, because it is made up of creatures, does not have enough perspective to make sense out of life. God, in His goodness, interprets reality for us. He came to Adam and

Eve and gave them His interpretation of their world, telling them what food was and what wasn't, what was safe and what was dangerous. As long as they trusted God's character and His counsel to them, they were safe.

The devil, knowing this, cast doubt on God's goodness and character, and tempted them to then disobey Him, insinuating that God was depriving them of something good.

The first question recorded in the Bible was the serpent questioning God and His ways, placing doubt in God's goodness: "Did God actually say, 'You shall not eat of any tree in the garden?'" (Gen. 3:1). Their dependence upon God was cast in the light of being a bad thing. The devil encouraged them to stop listening to God, to stop trusting His voice, and tempted them instead to listen to him, or rather, to trust themselves and decide what was good or evil for themselves.

In a word, he encouraged them to stop worshiping God. Now (and this is important) just because they stopped worshiping God, *it doesn't mean they ceased to worship*. Instead of listening to God's voice, they would instead trust in their own wisdom to decide what is good and evil. When one does that, they begin to look at creation to fulfill their desires for good and to avoid what they believe is evil. When one ceases to believe that pleasing and trusting God is the foundation of their life, they are open to listening to other's opinions on what is good and evil and will let those ideas shape how they think, live and act.

The world is then full of voices telling one where to find happiness, meaning, purpose and how to avoid suffering. When one ceases to worship God, they transfer that worship, ultimately, to themselves and to their own version of what will make them happy. That which we believe will bring us happiness will be different for each of us, shaped by the voices we listen to and how we interpret and make sense of our lives.

We are all worshipers, so the question is: What are you tempted to worship? It could be money, success, relationships, beauty or anything we value more than what the Lord has for us. Romans 1:25 shows us that, from the very beginning of creation, we are prone to look for value and meaning outside of our Creator: "... because they exchanged the truth about God for a lie and worshiped and served the creature rather than the Creator ..."

WHOSE IMAGE?

Does Scripture have anything to say about image? Anyone reasonably familiar with the Scriptures will know that it does. From the same creation account in Genesis 1-2, where it describes the creation of Adam and Eve, it states that God formed them in His own image, male and female He created them. Much ink has been spilled over the centuries about what this could mean, much of it centered around a certain quality humans possess (for example, some suggest the image of God is seen in humanity's capacity for rationality as compared to animals). In the Ancient Near East, however, the concept of an image was intimately wrapped up with worship. In Ancient Near Eastern religions, gods were thought to live in a garden or on top of a mountain, sometimes both. A temple would be built and an image of the god would be placed in the temple to represent the god. The thought was that a religious ceremony would be held where the people would "open the nostrils" of the god and the god would then enter into the idol or image and dwell there. The idol, then, represented the god.

In the biblical account of the creation of humanity, God creates the Garden of Eden, which acts as His temple, and then He creates human beings and breathes into them the breath of life. Men and women, then, are to represent God. They are made in the image of God. You and I are then tasked with participating in God's work of filling and ordering the world, just like God did in creating the world from what was formerly empty and void. Our calling in life is to image God, represent Him in the world, doing His work. This is where we get our purpose and identity from. We do this by listening to His voice, obeying Him; in a word, worshiping Him.

So, what does this have to do with body image? EVERYTHING!

One of the key points here is that the one to whom you listen, whose counsel and interpretation of reality you follow, will shape where you find your meaning, worth, and identity. Only our Creator should define those things, and He rightly does, *as long as we are listening to His voice and worshiping Him.*

So, as worshipers, we will image the god we worship. Our lives reflect what is important to us, what we value, and what we pursue. In the example with Katie, her life reflected the importance of her appearance and that importance played out in how she ate, how she dressed, how she spent her time online, her relationships, how she viewed herself and others, and how she interacted socially.

Jesus is called THE image of God. He said, when you've seen me, you've seen the Father. What did He mean? Jesus perfectly reveals the Father. As John 1:18 puts it, "who is at the Father's side, he has made him known." Jesus loved the Father and lived to do His will. He worshiped him, listened to Him and obeyed Him, saying, "I only do what the Father has shown me" (John 5:16-20) As an image bearer then, He looks like the One whom He worshiped. His whole life was directed to doing what the Father wanted.

As Christians, literally "little Christs" we are to do the same. Our calling in life is to listen to the Father, worship Him, and reflect His character and will in the world. That is our identity, calling, and purpose in life. As long as we listen to Him, love Him, and worship Him first, we will image Him to the world. We will look like Him. That is an image to aspire to, and one that is within our grasp. That will be reflected in how we live, how we spend our time, how we evaluate ourselves, and how we evaluate others.

In addition, this reality can never be taken from us. If we serve an image formed from the world's definition, we will lose it through aging, injury, disfigurement, and, ultimately, death. However, if we pursue pleasing the Lord, who we become in the process will never fade away. This life is about preparation for the age to come, the coming of the kingdom of God. We will be co-rulers with Jesus in His kingdom. That will never be taken from us. That is a calling, purpose, and identity that will never disappoint.

MAIN POINT

Christ is the image we are to pursue. Whom you listen to, whose counsel and interpretation of reality you follow, will shape where you find your meaning, worth, and identity.

REFLECTION QUESTIONS

- Why do you think the serpent was able to put doubt in Eve's mind so easily?
- What are ways you might doubt God's goodness?
- Can you identify things you are strongly tempted to worship? In what ways might they become idols in your life?

3. It Touches Us All

To varying degrees, we have all felt the struggle. We are keenly aware of the value society places on the attractive, athletic, successful, and seemingly perfect. We can all be lured into believing that to attain such things gives us greater worth or purpose.

- Do you ever catch yourself comparing your appearance to those around you?
- Find yourself on social media measuring your clothes, your shape, your possessions, or your performance to others?
- Attempt to alter things you don't like about your appearance?
- Feel flawed or imperfect due to your size or height?
- Avoid social situations due to insecurity about your looks?
- Feel shame over not being perfect or attractive enough?

- Value someone over others because they were attractive?
- Invest a great deal of time trying to improve your looks or shape?
- Have a love/hate relationship with the mirror?

Our battle with the mirror can shape a moment, a day, a lifetime – and become our identity. Does your battle with the mirror shape the way you feel about yourself from day to day? You can wake up feeling good about yourself, only to look in the mirror and notice a pimple, a wrinkle, or the bags under your eyes, and instantly, your mood has shifted. You can be content with your clothes, only to jump on social media and notice that someone else has better, newer, more expensive taste and style. You become convinced you fall short, leading you to chasing an elusive image of perfection.

Ask yourself: does my appearance affect the way I feel about myself? Do you find it regularly guides your behavior or choices? If so, you are learning that your daily habits reflect your functional beliefs. For example, do you find yourself upset if you are having a bad hair day? Do you feel "off" or grumpy when you can't get to the gym, or a comment is made about your appearance? Taking pride in your appearance and maintaining a healthy lifestyle clearly are not wrong; it is the *degree to which you allow those activities to dictate your worth that can be problematic.*

It is a pursuit of an ideal image, and it is a pursuit that deceives you. It promises pleasure and happiness but ensnares you and delivers heartache. God's Word warns us of its emptiness: "Charm is deceitful, and beauty is vain, but a woman who fears the LORD is to be praised" (Prov. 31:30). The pursuit is in vain, but there is genuine affirmation and praise to be found in the fear of the Lord. It is the fear of the Lord that fulfills; delighting in the One whom we were created to please.

When we find our worth in anything apart from the One who created us, it can lead to all kinds of empty and vain pursuits: unrealistic standards, perfectionism, materialism, love of beauty, body dysmorphia, obsessive social media use, eating disorders and much more. We fill our days with hollow pursuits and, in the end, it leaves us empty.

The Lord formed you exactly the way He wanted you: you are His masterpiece. Your Creator says you are fearfully and wonderfully made. He knit you together. He calls you by name and says you are His child (Isa. 43:1). This world tells you to find your worth in what it has to offer. People will judge and label you. They will try to convince you to be like them.

For you formed my inward parts;
you knitted me together in my
mother's womb.
I praise you, for I am fearfully and
wonderfully made.
Wonderful are your works;
my soul knows it very well.
(Ps. 139:13-14)

You can trust your Creator.
You are not a mistake.
Don't believe the lie.

MAIN POINT

There will always be people, things, and culture threatening to define you and tell you where to find worth. The only thing that will satisfy you is resting in God's good design.

QUESTIONS FOR REFLECTION

- What are things you rely on to make you feel good about your appearance?

- What do those things do for you, and why?
- How do you view yourself?
- How does God view you and how should that shape your perception?
- Why do you think it is so hard?

4. Mirrors Lie and Mirrors Isolate

Body image struggles are akin to living in a room full of mirrors. All you can see is what is reflecting back at you. You struggle to see beyond the mirror in front of you. It is always staring you in the eye, exposing your flaws, making you more self-focused. You find yourself unable to see beyond how others might be viewing you. Slowly, you become enslaved to the image that is displayed. Every time you leave your home, you are faced with how the world around you perceives you: every interaction, every relationship, every success and every failure.

Not only is the struggle like you are living in a room full of mirrors, but the image staring back at you is often distorted. Do you know what a "carnival mirror" is? They are mirrors made to distort the image in front of them, making one person extraordinarily tall and thin, another short and five feet wide, distorting you into something unrecognizable.

The more you and I fixate on our appearance, the more our own self-perception becomes distorted, like a carnival mirror. You cannot accurately see your flaws or strengths, everything is altered and disfigured. You lose the ability to truly evaluate yourself, and find yourself consumed with trying to create, or re-create, a "better" image. Perhaps what is even more dangerous has your worship shifted; you've allowed a graven image to be your idol?

When you live surrounded by mirrors, it impacts all your relationships by preventing you from being truly known. You are engulfed and fixated on your own self-perception. It isolates you from others because you are more invested in hiding flaws and keeping up appearances. Like a wall that prevents us from seeing beyond ourselves and inhibiting our view, our faulty self-perception hinders vulnerability and genuine relationship. The fear of rejection, of not being good enough, the desire for admiration keeps the stakes too high to risk being transparent – all contribute to this fear. It becomes a pattern of striving after admiration, more than to be truly known.

It isn't until we learn to find our worth in Christ that we can know genuine love and acceptance.

COMPARISON ALSO SEPARATES

Living before the mirror puts you in constant comparison to those around you. Comparison breeds lies; lies we believe both about ourselves and others. When we fall into comparison, we shift our focus from honest evaluation to competing against other people. They either will become a threat to us or a measuring stick. It is impossible to love others genuinely when we see them as a rival. Comparison gives rise to jealousy, robbing us of finding joy in the accomplishments of our peers.

The Bible acknowledges that great and small exist. There are the impressive and un-impressive in stature, appearances, giftings, or position. Society takes things such as education, possessions, fame, achievements, and looks, then uses them as ladders to rank one another. Even within churches, we can use things such as ministry accomplishments, marital status, lifestyle, or our children to rank one another.

The problem is when we use those differences to evaluate someone's worth. We turn each other into yardsticks, always holding ourselves up to the life of others; either leaving us to feel inadequate or we think ourselves superior. How quickly a God-ordained difference becomes a tool we use to judge each other.

Max Lucado illustrates this well in his book, *You Are Special*. It is a story about a town of wooden people who go around placing grey dots or star stickers on one another all day long. Every day, the small wooden people do the same thing: stick either gold stars or gray dots on one another. The pretty and talented ones always get stars. But the ones like Punchinello, who are not as talented or don't look as attractive, are given grey dots, and it shapes how others see him and how he sees himself. Then he meets one who has no stickers; she doesn't carry anyone's marks on her. She points him to their maker, the woodcarver Eli, who tells him the stickers only stick if you let them. His worth comes from his maker, not what other people say about him. The story emphasizes that others will try to label us. Eli the woodcarver helps Punchinello understand how special he is – no matter what others may think.[1] It's a message for all of us: Regardless of how the world evaluates you,

---

1. Max Lucado, *You Are Special* (Oxford: Lion Hudson, 2005).

you are God's workmanship, and that is what gives you value.

The mirrors we build prevent meaningful relationships; they quite literally isolate us. We become obsessed with self, with our own image, or what we believe others think about our image. This, in turn, leaves little room for care or concerns for others. The battle with the mirror makes us self-absorbed and unable to see the needs of others. We become obsessed with self and there is little room for concern for others. You will seek to be admired, more than to be known.

As Paul tells us in Philippians 2:3-4: "Do nothing from selfish ambition or conceit, but in humility count others more significant than yourselves. Let each of you look not only to his own interests, but also to the interests of others." The text is not telling you to have a low esteem of yourself. The answer isn't to think poorly of yourself, but rather to think about yourself less altogether and to look outward towards others. In *The Freedom of Self-Forgetfulness*, Tim Keller shares that freedom is not found is shallow outward change, but from an internal change of posture. There is no room for self-condemnation. In a world where pleasing people and self-promotion reign, true freedom can only come from self-forgetfulness.[2]

Are you trying to live for the applause of others? Are you striving after an ever-changing ideal of beauty and perfection? We can inadvertently build our own room full of mirrors, so caught up in the illusion it creates, that we find ourselves incapable of finding the way out. It becomes a prison of our own doing.

MAIN POINT

Living for appearance isolates and prevents us from knowing and being known by others.

REFLECTION QUESTIONS

- How do you think the world views you?
- What kind of labels do you think you are given (or fear being given) by others?
- What are ways you are afraid of being vulnerable or real with others? Why?
- What would happen if you took the risk to be real and transparent?

---

2   Tim Keller, *The Freedom of Self-Forgetfulness: The Path to True Christian Joy* (Lancashire: 10Publishing, 2012).

5. The Illusion

In *The Weight of Glory*, C.S. Lewis illustrates our struggle with self-worship: "And that is enough to raise your thoughts to what may happen when the redeemed soul, beyond all hope and nearly beyond belief, learns at last that she has pleased Him whom she was created to please. There will be no room for vanity then. She will be free from the miserable illusion that it is her doing. With no taint of what we should now call self-approval she will most innocently rejoice in the thing that God has made her to be, and the moment which heals her old inferiority complex forever will also drown her pride ... Perfect humility dispenses with modesty."[1] Living before the mirror, the approval of self or others, is indeed a miserable illusion. It promises happiness, self-love, and affirmation,

1   C.S. Lewis, *The Weight of Glory*, (London: Harper-Collins, 1980), p. 38.

yet it is an empty promise. Only in Christ can we find real freedom from the prison of the worldly affirmation.

Think about the beauty industry: its primary purpose is to sell products. To accomplish this, we must be convinced that we cannot be complete without the item they are selling. We are faced with a barrage of subliminal messages about who we are and what we should be. This creates an image of what beauty and perfection look like, creating a strong need to purchase products to fit societal ideals. Marketing, magazines, social media sites, billboards, fashion centers, and more: all shape and normalize a standard of beauty. By creating an ideal and convincing women that any individual product can achieve that ideal, they are developing a need and offering a solution.

The industry does not want to convince you that you are good enough; they want to convince you that you *can* be good enough – if you buy what they are selling.

It is not only selling you merchandise but values, morals, ideals of romance, love, and sexuality. Society promotes what it wants you to believe is desirable and socially acceptable, proselytizing you to believe that what they offer is normal and provides happiness.

Culture creates a perception of what is normal. Women's bodies are objectified and distorted in media, which attempts to reflect how we should view our own bodies. These are ideals that even most models admit they are unable to attain. Computer retouching is used to thin down models, add more curves, make hair thicker, longer, eyes closer together, lips fuller. It is commonplace to have models so retouched, they admit to wishing they looked like the image they've been turned into. With AI and computer retouching, it is now possible that you can view a picture of a model that does not exist. Computers make it achievable to create models manufactured with body parts of dozens of individuals and crafted to be an image of beauty for which you should strive.

The perfect North American fashion model is 5 foot 8 inches and weighs 115 lbs. However, the average North American woman is 5 foot 3 inches and weighs 144 lbs. The perfect model weighs 23 per cent less than the average woman. The message given to women by the fashion, diet, and media industries is that we're never good enough. This leads young women to deprive themselves constantly and continually fight against the natural size of their bodies.

When this happens, the effects can vary from occasional dieting to serious eating disorders, from extreme depression to dangerous weight loss surgery. Ninety to ninety-five per cent of people with eating disorders are women. Moreover, many statistics show that most women have some degree of body image dissatisfaction. Little girls at nine years old— and as young as four or five—are expressing a wish to diet.

Constant images of beautiful women who are dangerously thin creates an allure. The media promotes a biologically unattainable ideal. The diet industry then promises to deliver it. Food becomes a tempting taboo, while plastic surgery has upped the stakes of perfection. We can see how an image creates an allure to shape what we should value.

For years, it was thought that primarily women wrestled with body image. However, we know that men also struggle with appearance. By and large, men are conditioned not to discuss their body image issues. Various research shows that males suffering from eating disorders or body image issues often experience depression and shame. Because of cultural preconceptions, men are expected to hide their insecurities, rather than confront them. Some examples of how this might manifest in men are:

- Continual comparison to others.
- Restrictive dieting or excessive attention to diet.
- Excessive exercise or weightlifting.
- Social withdrawal.
- Use of steroids.
- Muscle dysmorphia (negative self-image and obsessive desire to be muscular).
- Seeking praise or approval from the opposite sex.

Matt was a college wrestler. He started in high school, and, like many wrestlers his age, he worked hard to gain muscle, get stronger, and lose weight in order to make weigh-in. He watched as his peers took extreme measures to prepare for competitions: they used saunas, dehydrated themselves, and had extreme dieting plans all to cut weight.

Matt wanted to fit in and keep up with his teammates, so he also began rigorous workouts, deprived himself of liquids, and would go a day or two without eating before weigh-ins. He and his buddies would all joke and bemoan their efforts, and Matt felt a camaraderie in his efforts. Matt and his friends spent time watching videos of elite athletes, learning tips and tricks on how to bulk up, while slimming down. This continued in college.

Between his eating habits and his exercise regime, Matt began to feel the toll on his health. He was constantly tired and exhausted, battling colds and fatigue. During the day he attended classes, but had trouble focusing and would forget information during exams. He'd find it hard to do well in his competitions as well, causing him to feel discouraged and frustrated.

He would compensate by working out more. He developed disordered eating patterns, starving and dehydrating himself before a match, then binging afterwards. Matt surfed social media, watching videos and trying to find ways to improve his strength and agility. His began letting other responsibilities slide: missing classes, skipping out on meetings, and avoiding family events.

Matt was caught in a cycle of anxiety and outward pressure to succeed. He found comfort and pleasure in the comments he got about his physique. Girls would pursue him, stroking his ego and soothing his insecurities. He began attending parties, staying up late and hooking up with girls. What started out as a desire to become a good athlete morphed into a drive to find identity in his appearance.

Though these issues may manifest differently in women, the themes are often similar and the results equally as destructive. Caught in one's own perceptions and insecurities, we struggle to see beyond the distorted image in the mirror we believe is being reflected back to us. We end up striving after an image the world puts before us.

The message is unmistakable: you are told that what's most important is how we look – and how we fall short. Advertisers surround us with images of ideal female beauty and young women learn very early that they must invest substantial amounts of time, energy, and money in efforts to achieve this ideal. When you and I fall short (and we will) because the ideal is based on absolute perfection, shame and worthlessness follow quickly behind.

Self-worth is defined by appearance, and we are encouraged to pursue doing everything we can to measure up. If you're constantly thinking about your appearance, you're falling into the lie that your worth is found in your outward appearance. Though it has been most familiar to girls and women, increasingly more boys and men also fall into this trap. Social media adds another avenue for us to compare ourselves to others.

A disordered value on body image does more than fixating on striving for an ideal, though that is problematic enough. It also increases the risk of engaging in unhealthy lifestyle behaviors, such as dieting or restrictive eating, over-exercising and other disordered eating or weight control behaviors. Regular dieting is a significant risk factor for developing an eating disorder. Food, created by God to be nourishing and a source of enjoyment and celebration, becomes something bad or taboo. The temptation to be re-creating our image over and over leads to all kinds of damage – and sometimes it is irreversible.

Body image struggles change the way you perceive and relate to your own body. They lead you down all kinds of self-destructive paths:

- sinking us deeper into shame through harmful coping mechanisms like self-harm, disordered eating, and abuse of alcohol or drugs.

- keeping us clinging to those uncomfortable comfort zones through hiding – and fixing hiding by avoiding events, situations, and activities where you don't want to be looked at.
- fixing us by trying to change our appearance in some way to cope with shame, whether that's through a liquid only detox, liposuction, or plastic surgery.
- limiting and restricting ourselves in unhealthy ways through food rituals and obsessions.

Body image struggles also lead to behaviors such as perfectionism, self-critical behaviors and thoughts, obsession with appearance and materialism, focus on consumerism, vanity, and self-worship. We become a people fixated on ourselves, unable to see outside of the mirror.

Women then measure their worth by the numbers on a scale and the pictures on the screen. The idea that external appearance is what defines us drives women to all kinds of destructive and superficial behaviors. As believers, when did we buy into this idea? When do we set aside all that Scripture has to say about our worth and identity and decide that the creative thing could deliver what we've always wanted? You must be aware that these images are a lie and mask them for what they truly are.

MAIN POINT

The world creates an image or ideal and persuades you to pursue it.

REFLECTION QUESTIONS

- What is the illusion the world presents to us?
- What makes it so tempting?
- What is the message of the beauty industry? What are they trying to do?
- How is the struggle similar for men and women? How is it different?
- Why do you think Christians fall into this trap as well?

6. Is the Answer More Self-Esteem?

How do you feel about your appearance right now? This very second, are you satisfied? Why or why not? Is rebuffing societal standards enough? Is having better self-esteem the solution? If you and I feel good about ourselves, will that be the answer to all our struggles?

Over the years, many began to call out the unrealistic and permanently harmful standard of body image that was being projected. Women and men alike were objectified, and this always leads to the dehumanizing of one another. People began challenging media to represent more diverse and authentic images of people along with a positive message. Many women began fighting back by rejecting culturally imposed beauty standards and replacing them with their own, individual version of beauty. Another positive change was the acknowledgement of the need for positive relationships and role models, particularly for young girls.

There have been many well-meaning companies and people advocating to improve women's body image by pushing the message that all women are beautiful, flaws and all. In advertising, more diverse women of color, age and body shape have been represented. Differences are celebrated, rather than marginalized. Freedom of individuality and the perception of what is beautiful has broadened to be more inclusive. It is a message of self-acceptance: you are beautiful the way you are. Love yourself more; accept yourself as you are; be okay with imperfections and your natural size.

Programs have formed in school and universities to address literacy in the media, counteracting the unrealistic standards; they encourage body satisfaction and good self-esteem. The message is to be kind to yourself, not fall for unrealistic standards and spend time with people who make you feel good about yourself. Bad advice?

The premise is that positive body image isn't just believing your body looks good; it's knowing your body is good regardless of how you look. Treat yourself well; love your body.

We all must have realistic standards, accept our shortcomings, and love ourselves more as we are. Sounds good, right? It is certainly better than living for the approval of others and always feeling inadequate. However, it isn't fixing the problem.

We are not only suffering because of the unattainable ways beauty is being defined, but because we are being defined by appearance at all. That was never meant to be the image we live for. It objectifies: you become a physical, mortal body first and individual person second. The fixation with positive body image still makes our appearance the issue; it still makes one's worth and value based on how we feel about our outward appearance. We are just exchanging one man-made image for another.

Any agenda for change must focus on the thoughts and desires of the heart. And it has to begin with God's standards of these things. The answer is not to focus more on ourselves and how we feel about ourselves, but to think about ourselves less and to know what a proper focus is. In many of these messages, there is still a mentality that you and I deserve happiness, good circumstances, and a good self-image. It tempts you and me to pursue good esteem for the sake of making ourselves feel better. We also are tempted to allow ourselves to be valued by what others value – or value about us. We look to what others find attractive or appealing and try to emulate it.

To place importance on external appearance is an age-old struggle of humanity. Consistently in Scripture, we see this struggle: people are discounted due to their position, size, age, status, or gender. Consider what the Lord said to Samuel, as He sent Samuel out to anoint a new king for Israel: "But the LORD said to Samuel, "Do not look on his appearance or on the height of his stature, because I have rejected him. For the LORD sees not as man sees: man looks on the outward appearance, but the LORD looks on the heart" (1 Sam. 16:7).

Value, importance, success, and beauty are not found in what is external, but in what is internal. The measure of an individual is found in their character, integrity, and their relationship with the Lord. The message in Scripture is clear: God will choose the least likely to do His will, and it is rarely the strongest, most beautiful, the most skilled, or the most eloquent. It is those who humbly find their identity and value in the Lord; those who find their worth and meaning in life based on what He says is important.

Rather than working to make sure more of our outward bodies are viewed as valuable, we should be focused on growing inward value as image bearers made in the image of a good Creator.

C.S. Lewis says this in *The Weight of Glory*: "It would seem that the Lord finds our desires not too strong, but too weak. We are half-hearted creatures, fooling about with drink and sex and ambition when infinite joy is offered to us. Like an ignorant child who wants to go on making mud pies in the slum because he cannot imagine what is meant by the offer of a holiday at the sea. We are far too easily pleased."

The problem isn't that you and I expect too much from God; it's that we often expect too little. We stare into mirrors that distort us, when the Lord offers an honest, accurate reflection. He has made you in His image and is committed to continue refining you into His image, but you find yourself chasing after images that are fleeting and shallow. We are willing to settle for the images this world tries to sell to us, but it is much like making mud pies in the slum. God offers us an identity that is richer, more beautiful and incapable of disappointing us.

Isaiah 55:2 says this: "Why spend your money on what is not bread, and your labor on what does not satisfy? Listen, listen to me, and eat what is good and your soul will delight in the richest of fare." Your Heavenly Father desires for you to be satisfied in Him.

WE ARE NOT OUR OWN

When we are driven by appearance, it often leads, as previously noted, to all kinds of unhealthy ways we treat our body. Perhaps you are an avid exerciser: you demonstrate great self-control and beat your body into submission for the purpose of excelling at a sport or conform your body into the desired image. It almost seems admirable, does it not? However, if you were honest, you'd admit that your motive was not so pious. You are being ruled by your passions: a certain look, public persona, or maybe desire to keep up with your peers. Maybe you struggle with an eating disorder; you swing between starving your body, to purging and making yourself sick. You look in the mirror and feel disgust, treating your body like it is your enemy. How you treat your body reveals what you really believe to be true.

There is another message culture places upon us, that goes against the message in Scripture, and that is: "My body, My choice." It is a refrain that is intended to represent the idea of personal bodily autonomy and freedom. It pronounces one's ownership and choice to do whatever they want with their bodies without any external regulation or restraint. There are Christians who have repeated this refrain as well, yet it is antithetical to the message and the work of Christ.

The reality is we do not have ultimate say or autonomy over ourselves. We are image-bearers and belong to Him who made us. "For you were bought with a price. So glorify God in your body" (1 Cor. 6:20). Your body is a temple of the Holy Spirit. To quote the Heidelberg catechism, "You are not your own."[1] You are a temple in which the Spirit of God resides. Therefore, how we maintain our body will either honor or dishonor the Lord. Like modern culture, the Corinthian culture often encouraged immorality, patterns of behavior and thought that impacted how they lived out their lives. Though Paul is speaking to the immoral lifestyle

---

1   Heidelberg Catechism, Q&A 1

being expressed, the principle can be applied here as well.

We are not to defile our bodies. We are not our own; we have been redeemed with the blood of Christ. His blood purchased us, redeemed us, and delivered us from the misery of our own bondage. The lies we believe about our appearance and body image issues enslave us and keep us in bondage; Christ came to rescue us and make us the dwelling place of His Spirit.

Rather than seeing it as a restriction on us, we must see that as a responsibility. We are called to steward our lives, including our bodies, in a way that honors Christ. You are no longer to walk in the ways of the world. We are not our own. We are called to be a living sacrifice, holy and pleasing to God (Rom. 12:1). In our bodies and behavior, we no longer strive to make ourselves beautiful; instead, we aim to reflect the beauty of Christ through us.

As believers, we are also redeemed from the lies we have believed about where life and happiness are found. In Scripture, we read things like: "Man does not live by bread alone, but man lives by every word that comes from the mouth of the LORD" (Deut. 8, Matt 4), or, "Be transformed by the renewing of your mind" (Rom 12:2).

Whom we listen to and what we believe will shape how we live, feel, and act. It will inform our day-to-day behavior. When we are believers, God's Spirit comes to dwell in us to transform our hearts, so we don't believe lies anymore about where life is found (being a certain size, looking a certain way, having so many followers, gaining affection/approval/love). The Spirit of God in us reorients how we live and act and where we find worth. Instead, we become like Christ, imaging Him and committed to do the Father's will. Christ spoke these words: "I have food to eat that you do not know about. My food is to do the will of him who sent me" (John 4:32-34). The disciples came back from town and were shocked to find Jesus speaking with a Samaritan woman. The disciples were convinced that Jesus just needed to eat something. Material things will not ultimately satisfy.

But Jesus was trying to communicate what will actually bring a deeper satisfaction in your soul: doing the Father's will. He is our daily bread, nourishing us and satisfying our soul. God's provision never runs dry and is always available to us; His mercies are new every morning.

You are God's temple; your identity is secure. He will never leave you, He will always provide for you, and He will satisfy your soul. You have been set free from the fear of man, from finding identity in your looks or worth in all that enslaves you. You have been bought with a price: walk in this freedom and honor the Lord with your body.

MAIN POINT

You are not your own; you belong to Him who made you. That truth should shape how you live.

REFLECTION QUESTIONS

- What is the solution culture tries to offer to the problem of distorted body image?
- Is it wrong to feel good about yourself or your accomplishments?
- What might be the danger?
- Are there ways you try to satisfy your soul apart from God? What are they?
- Are you willing to let go of those things?
- How would living to do the Father's will satisfy? What might that look like?

7. Where Does Real Beauty Come From?

Your beauty should not come from outward adornment, such as elaborate hairstyles and the wearing of gold jewelry or fine clothes. Rather, it should be that of your inner self, the unfading beauty of a gentle and quiet spirit, which is of great worth in God's sight. (1 Pet. 3:3-4 NIV)

Have you ever met someone whom at first glance strikes you as very pretty or handsome? They may be attractive, charismatic, or impressive in stature. However, as you begin to get to know them, you find out that they are self-centered, unkind, arrogant, greedy, and self-absorbed. The more you interact with them, the less attractive they become to you; perhaps they even become repulsive to be around.

Jesus makes a similar indictment towards the Pharisees and religious leaders, calling them whitewashed tombs who look beautiful on the outside, but are filled on the inside with dead people's bones and all sorts of impurity (Matt. 23:27). We can do everything to present ourselves one way outwardly, but God knows the heart of every human.

Imagine the movies where corpses rise from the grave and go around devouring the living. You have the dead, seeking to come back to life by devouring those around then. I often think our striving for beauty and youth and perfection is just that: the dead devouring and comparing in hopes of gaining life from it. We are living corpses: outwardly aging, losing our faculties, dying, yet we spend all our time chasing after things that we think will bring us life.

We are striving after that which will not satisfy, will not make us any younger, will not keep age and wrinkles and physical deterioration from finding us. It promises something real, but only delivers death. What profit is it to us if we gain beauty, wealth, possessions, admiration? We think it will satisfy, but we will lose something far greater. As Jesus asks in Matthew 16:26, "For what will it profit a man if he gains the whole world and forfeits his soul?

WHAT ABOUT THE "UNATTRACTIVE"?

Now, consider the person who at first glance is not physically appealing. They may be unattractive or difficult to look at. Maybe it's due to age, gray hair and wrinkles abound, muscles weaken, time and circumstances have not aged them well. Others experience tragic accidents where their bodies and faces are forever scarred or they are missing limbs. By all outward appearance, they're considered unsightly.

However, as you begin to interact with them you are struck by their friendly mannerism and kind disposition. They treat people with respect; there is no arrogance or guile in them. They may not be physically good-looking, but they are attractive in speech and action. They turn their liabilities into assets and, rather than focusing on themselves, they help others who are in need, and they make you feel valued.

This illustrates how the world focuses and assesses people based on the external. God emphasizes the internal. Beauty fades, but character and godliness grow and transform how we see one another. Our vision changes and we begin to see what is real and truly beautiful.

In the children's book, *The Velveteen Rabbit*, there is a charming exchange between two toys, the Rabbit and the Skin Horse. about what it means to become real.

"What is REAL?" asked the Rabbit one day, when they were lying side by side near the nursery fender, before Nana came to tidy the room. "Does it mean having things that buzz inside you and a stick-out handle?"

"Real isn't how you are made," said the Skin Horse. "It's a thing that happens to you. When a child loves you for a long, long time, not just to play with, but REALLY loves you, then you become Real."

"Does it hurt?" asked the Rabbit.

"Sometimes," said the Skin Horse, for he was always truthful. "When you are Real you don't mind being hurt."

"Does it happen all at once, like being wound up," he asked, "or bit by bit?"

"It doesn't happen all at once," said the Skin Horse. "You become. It takes a long time. That's why it doesn't often happen to people who break easily, or have sharp edges, or

who have to be carefully kept. Generally, by the time you are Real, most of your hair has been loved off, and your eyes drop out and you get loose in the joints and very shabby. But these things don't matter at all, because once you are Real you can't be ugly, except to people who don't understand."[1]

Something much more profound is being suggested in this sweet exchange than may at first be recognized. It is that being loved, truly loved, is what makes one real and beautiful. This often happens over time, in the fading away of outward beauty and perfection. It is a process and journey to becoming. Beauty comes from within, from the character of an individual. We often find it comes over time: with maturity, experience, age (and often wrinkles), beauty emerges as we let go of all that is temporary and begin to understand what is of eternal value.

As one writer said: "She was beautiful, but not like those girls in the magazines. She was beautiful for the way she thought. She was beautiful for the sparkle in her eyes when she talked about something she loved. She

---

1   Margery Williams, *The Velveteen Rabbit*, (Greenwood: Suzeteo Enterprises, 2017), p.13.

was beautiful for her ability to make other people smile, even if she was sad. No, she wasn't beautiful for something as temporary as her looks. She was beautiful, deep down to her soul."[2]

It is a similar sentiment: when we look beyond the outward facade, the attractive or unattractive face, something more real emerges. Beauty is defined by character, the soul of a person. Scripture takes it further: beauty is found and unfading in the one who is being transformed into Christlikeness.

Two Corinthians 4:16 put it this way:

So we do not lose heart. Though our outer self is wasting away, our inner self is being renewed day by day.

Everything that pertains to the physical person is perishing. We are living corpses, decaying outwardly. Yet inwardly, our spiritual life is being renewed again and again, day by day. We continue to grow and to be transformed into the likeness of Christ. The inward man is the person who belongs to Christ and we

---

2   This quote is often attributed to F. Scott Fitzgerald but its authorship is harder to pin down.

are progressively being transformed into the image of Christ.

Two Corinthians 4:17-18 takes it a step further:

For this light momentary affliction is prep-aring for us an eternal weight of glory beyond all comparison, as we look not to the things that are seen but to the things that are unseen. For the things that are seen are transient, but the things that are unseen are eternal.

Earlier, we discussed that it is not about the external but the internal. We see here that it is ultimately about the eternal. We are outwardly wasting away, yet inwardly being transformed into something much more beautiful. Much more real than anything this earth has to offer. We do not lose heart because we fix our eyes on what is eternal.

C.S. Lewis once wrote, "For a few minutes we had the illusion of belonging to that world. Now we wake to find that there is no such thing. We have been mere spectators."[3]

---

3   C.S. Lewis, *Mere Christianity,* (San Francisco, Harper One, 2001).

God, who is the creator of all things, who is in all things and through whom all things exist (Rom. 12:36), establishes what is real and anything that is superficial or a facade will fade away.

We are transformed by the love of God. We are not just changed or made real; we are made new in Christ. We are quite literally a new creation (2 Cor. 5:17). The old has gone, the new has come. When we let go of all vain pursuits and give ourselves over to the Lord, whom we were meant to please, His love begins to transform us into something far more beautiful and real.

MAIN POINT

Beauty is found in the inner person; we are living in light of eternity.

REFLECTION QUESTIONS

- Is it wrong to find someone attractive or unattractive? Why or why not?
- How do your own biases inform how you judge or view others?
- What does Scripture say about beauty? How is it defined?
- What does it mean to live for the eternal?

8. How Do We Change?

———

Do you have a favorite Bible verse? Have you ever given thought to that before? All of God's Word is a treasure, but sometimes there are verses that resonate with us differently. One of my favorite passages of Scripture is found in 2 Corinthians 4:7, which says: "But we have this treasure in jars of clay, to show that the surpassing power belongs to God and not to us."

Picture a beautiful oriental vase. It is intricate, beautiful, colorful, attractive to look at and placed upon a mantel for all to admire. Now imagine next to it, an old, rough, clay pot; it has cracks and perhaps a hole in it. Which will you be drawn to? Most likely, the beautiful vase.

Often, in the Christian life, we believe what God requires of us is to be the vase, to be this perfect Christian: without flaws, proper, put together, articulate, and never struggling. The moment a flaw emerges, we quickly get out the paint and gloss and try to cover it up. But 2 Corinthians gives us a different image to aspire to. We are entreated to be jars of clay, imperfect, unpretentious, humbled, and weak. Why? "… to show that the surpassing power belongs to God and not to us." There is freedom in the flaws. It is in the brokenness and flaws that Christ shines all the more brightly in us.

Imagine placing a light in the beautiful vase, and one in the cracked, imperfect jar of clay, then turn off the lights. Where will the light shine the brightest? Your eyes will likely be drawn to the jar of clay, where light is pouring out of the cracks and the holes in the midst of the darkness. That is what God does in and through you. He takes your struggles and weaknesses and demonstrates His power. His strength will be made perfect in and through us.

Christ is seen in us when we stop competing for attention. The less we are consumed with the exterior presentation and the more we focus on who and what captures our hearts, the more truly beautiful we become.

Identity is not found in appearance, but in a person: Jesus Christ.

For he shall grow up before him as a tender plant, and as a root out of a dry ground: he hath no form nor comeliness; and when we shall see him, there is no beauty that we should desire him. He is despised and rejected of men; a man of sorrows and acquainted with grief: and we hid as it were our faces from him; he was despised, and we esteemed him not (Isa. 53:2-3 KJV).

Scripture often turns our perceptions and our expectations upside down. Man looks at the outward appearance; God looks at the heart. Man expected Christ to come as a King, but He came as a baby. Christ came not as valiant knight riding in on chariots in all His glory. He came not as a handsome prince that we would all envy. Rather, He came as a suffering servant, despised, having "no beauty that we should desire him" (Isa. 53:2).

We think we must become impressive in order for the Lord to use us or find us worthy, but we forget that it is in Him we become worthy, accepted, and more than enough.

Christ modeled how to live in this world and not find identity in it. He refused to accept the labels people tried to place upon Him. Rather, He was a perfect reflection of the image we were to model, that our hearts would be captured by Him.

We are complete when we are ruled by the same desires that ruled Him. No one changes simply by choosing to stop wanting what rules them. They change when what is most important to them changes. They change because they choose to be ruled by other desires. Jesus was controlled by a devotion to pleasing His Father. He worshiped and trusted Him. Jesus, as an image bearer, perfectly reflected the Father's character by trusting Him and walking out His trust in obedience.

Jesus perfectly images the Father. Because He did so, Jesus could say, "when you've seen me, you've seen the Father" (John 14:9). As we are ruled by the same trust and desire to please God, we will begin to live in new ways; people will then begin to see God shining through us, through our brokenness. We will begin to look like our Father, imaging Him. We begin to change when we begin to be ruled by new desires, the same desires Jesus had.

Finding your identity and satisfaction in the One who made you brings great peace and acceptance. He knows you and is for you. Every area of life transforms into something beautiful as a result of your relationship with the Lord.

Consider what God says about you:

- You are His workmanship (Eph. 2:10).
- God does not judge you by outward appearance but looks on the heart (1 Sam. 16:7).
- You are made in His own image (Gen. 1:27).
- You are a chosen race, a royal priesthood, a holy nation, a person for His own possession (1 Peter 2:9).
- You are a new creation (2 Cor. 5:17).
- You were formed by Him and He knit you together in your mother's womb (Ps. 139:13).
- You are of more value than many sparrows (Luke 12:7).
- He began a good work in you and will bring it to completion (Phil. 1:6).
- You are being transformed into His image (2 Cor. 3:18).
- He loves you with an everlasting love (Jer. 31:1).
- He formed you in the womb and knew you before you were born (Jer. 1:5).

THE WORK OF THE SPIRIT IN US

And I will ask the Father, and he will give you another Helper, to be with you forever. (John 14:16)

The Holy Spirit is there to help us. "Likewise the Spirit helps us in our weakness. For we do not know what to pray for as we ought, but the Spirit himself intercedes for us with groanings too deep for words" (Rom. 8:26).

It is tempting to hear all of this and begin formulating a "How I can I do this" mentality. You might try mustering up the moral fortitude to be different, to not care what labels the world tries to give you. You might look for ways to be more Christlike, less self-consumed, more focused on others. There are high expectations to image Jesus Christ that requires far more than you and I have within ourselves. Yet still, our first reaction is often to attempt some type of formula for becoming what God asks of us.

When this happens, you miss something foundational. What God has asked of you and me can never be accomplished by sheer human grit and determination. This cuts to the heart of why we often fail when we are struggling with our body image, identity, or giving up unhealthy habits or patterns of sin in our life.

Much of what we do in our daily Christian life flows from a self-generated morally-controlled heart. We attempt to express personal holiness through strength of character or a natural desire to be good.

When we understand the gospel, we realize that we are given a Helper. He gives us help to find the grace to change, so we are not at the mercy of our own abilities. We are liberated from ourselves. This liberation begins with the work of the Spirit. It progresses over time as our desires begin to change. The Spirit also helps us to recognize the lies we have believed that have shaped our lives. He replaces them with truth. As Jesus says, "But the Helper, the Holy Spirit, whom the Father will send in my name, he will teach you all things and bring to your remembrance all that I have said to you" (John 14:26).

There is a difference between a human-controlled heart versus the Spirit-transformed heart. In life, self-generated goodness will not carry us far. We are not capable of any good apart from Christ's life inside us. Only a Spirit-renewed heart, one that clings to grace, can overcome evil with good. When the Spirit thrives in us, we can trust He will do a good work in us. Christ enables us to lay down my life and our rights and find value and purpose in Him. When we recognize the grace we have received, this also begins to create new desires, to please and move toward the Father in trust and love and gratitude.

God is at work perfecting Himself in you, no matter what you have done, or how you have struggled. He does not waste anything in your life. He has sent you a Comforter and a Helper and He is creating a new heart, a new life, for you. We must allow the Holy Spirit to move in our lives so that we can be transformed and will be empowered and to live in humble obedience. Then the Spirit will equip us for every good work.

MAIN POINT

God has given you His Spirit to do the work in your life.

REFLECTION QUESTIONS

- Are there ways you have tried to change on your own? What happened?

- Have you ever felt too far gone, or incapable of change?
- What does it mean that God is perfecting us?
- What does the Spirit of God do for us? What can He do for you?

9. Is it Wrong to Care About Appearance?

So, if true beauty is about the internal character of a person, not the outward form, is it wrong or sinful to put effort into our appearance? If charm is deceptive and beauty fleeting – should I avoid drawing any attention to myself? Is it sinful? No, in fact, it is good when not corrupted by sin and idolatry. A desire for beauty is not wrong, unless it rules us. It is a good thing but not an *ultimately* good thing.

A stoic view perceives beauty as corrupt and vain. It assumes that anything that draws attention to appearance is wrong. Therefore, we must refrain from anything that draws attention to us. Godliness is defined by a mundane, colorless expression. This produces a legalism that limits us and also defines us harshly by outward appearance. Modesty is no longer seen simply as a form of dress, but as a disposition of character. A stoic view limits us, just like a godless view does.

God is the author of beauty and creativity. You cannot look at creation without bumping into this truth everywhere you turn. After creating the world, He looked back and declared it good. All true beauty, that is rightly ordered, acts as a mirror, pointing us back to the Creator. He is the author of it and He delights in His creation, including His people. No two are alike, we are meant to express ourselves. Our individuality can be a celebration, rather than each of us forced into a clone like existence.

God calls us His masterpiece and His workmanship. He uses our gifts and talents, our assets, strengths, and even our flaws – all for His glory and for our good. In implicit and explicit ways, the Bible demonstrates that beauty is created by God and for His good pleasure. The best the world could offer is an image that confines, suppresses, and distorts all that is meant to be real and genuine.

The Bible models God's sovereignty, good-ness, and creative liberty in all of creation, as well as each of us individually. No two are alike, nor are we meant to be alike. There is tremendous freedom in self-expression when we use it to point back to the One who made us. We find liberty and freedom to express our uniqueness for it is not driven by self-promotion, but appropriately brings glory to the God of creation. It frees us towards godly self-expression. The world is what tries to press us all into a rigid narrow definition of beauty. God delights in beauty, in all of its varied expressions.

Acceptance is no longer found in public opinion, but in our personal relationship with the Lord. Self-expression, then, is uninhibited because it is *rightly ordered*. It is rightly ordered because the quest for beauty is no longer preeminent but in submission to a greater desire to please God. It is a picture of redemption that frees us from the bonds of human approval and entices us to delight in all that is purely beautiful and holy.

The goal of self-expression should be to mirror Christ. We reflect His image in us for the world to see.

MAIN POINT

Relationship with Christ does not limit you, but rather it liberates you towards godly self-expression.

REFLECTION QUESTIONS

- Think through the many ways God demonstrates He is the creator of beauty. List as many as you can.
- Knowing this, in what ways does it free you towards self-expression?
- Consider ways this may be demonstrated in your life. Are there changes you would make?

Conclusion: This Changes our Relationships

When we change, our relationships change. Relationships are no longer a threat or a measuring stick but instead foster honesty, authenticity, and meaningful connection. The mirrors are shattered, the walls are broken down. You can begin investing in knowing others and being known. Rather than trying to create uniformity, genuine community celebrates differences and appreciates one another's giftings and individuality. We will not stand in judgment of each other; we will encourage one another in weakness, spur each other towards change, and lift each other up when one is struggling.

B.B. Warfield once wrote this about Jesus:

Christ was led by His love for others into the world, to forget Himself in the needs of others, to sacrifice self once for all upon the alter of sympathy. Self-sacrifice brought Christ into the world. And self-sacrifice will lead us, His followers, not away from but into the midst of men. Wherever men suffer, there will be comfort. Wherever men strive, there will we be to help. Whenever men fail, there will we be to uplift. Whenever men succeed, there will we be to rejoice. Self-sacrifice means not indifference to our times and our fellows: it means absorption in them. It means forgetfulness of self in others. It means entering into every man's hopes and fears, longings and despairs: it means many-sidedness of spirit, multiform activity, multiplicity of sympathies. It means richness of development. It means not that we should live one life, but a thousand lives – binding ourselves to a thousand souls by the filaments of so loving a sympathy that their lives become ours.

It means that all the experiences of men shall smite our souls and shall beat and batter these stubborn hearts of ours into fitness for their heavenly home. It is, after all, then, the path to the highest possible development, by which alone we can be made truly men.[1]

---

1   B.B. Warfield, "Imitating the Incarnation" in The Savior of the World, (Edinburgh: Banner of Truth Trust, 1991), pp. 247-70.

To be changed into the image of Christ means a forgetting of self, self-sacrifice, humility, and looking to the good of others. As Christ was moved out of sacrificial love, so must we be. The gospel changes you, and it changes your relationships. You were not created to be isolated, but to be in loving, healthy community.

Finding your identity in Christ frees you to move outward, rather than be inwardly self-absorbed. You do not need to walk through your struggle alone. Galatians 6:2 calls us to bear one another's burdens. There never needs to be a reason you are embarrassed or ashamed of the way you are affected by the world's sin and brokenness. We are all impacted. When we allow ourselves to feel vulnerable and open about struggles, we find that godly relationships can foster our faith in God and our ability to overcome our battle with the mirror.

The community of believers is designed to help each other and shoulder one another's burdens. When a load becomes too heavy for one person, know there are people who understand and can help. If you find yourself feeling overcome by the weight of your struggle, share it with wise, trusted individuals. The added strength and encouragement of others is often the difference between pressing on and giving up.

MAIN POINT

A relationship with Christ changes your other relationships in meaningful ways.

REFLECTION QUESTIONS

- How has body image issues hindered relationships in your life?
- How does this (or could it) change your relationships?
- What are ways you can move towards community and begin sharing your story?

Appendix A: Next Steps

ASK THE LORD FOR HELP

Confess the ways you struggle with body image, performance, identity, and the like. He cares deeply for you. Psalm 46:1 says "… God is a very present help in trouble." You can call out to Him and make your requests known to Him. Share your heart, your struggles, your needs, and your fears. He will meet you where you are, enter in and let Him help you.

GET INTO COMMUNITY

It is tempting to separate from others when you are struggling, but as we discussed, it is important to be in a church community. When you are tempted to believe the illusion, a healthy, godly community reflects back to you what is true, and right, and good. Start with a church, small group or Bible study and begin to study God's Word. Get to know others and let them get to know you.

REACH OUT FOR MATURE HELP

You do not need to struggle alone. Find mature, wise people to walk alongside you, help you see clearly, and speak truth into your life. Maybe it is a parent, a ministry leader, or sometimes it is helpful to have a mentor who has walked further down the road than you have. You may find you need more help and your struggle has become too big for you. Consider when you may need a counselor, or someone more trained in the area of body image; don't be afraid to get a professional involved.

REST IN GOD'S LOVE

The more you know what God and His Word says about your life, the more you will find your identity in what He says is true. You are made in His image; let His power shine all the more brightly in you. When you are weak, He is strong. He is a loving shepherd who watches over you.

REJECT THE LABELS

Be vigilant to recognize the lies and labels that this world will try to place upon you. What was once a fear of the labels others put on you – or you put on yourself – will be replaced with a peace that you never imagined you could find. The more you trust in His love, the less you will be driven by what others think.

Appendix B: Further Reading

Tim Keller, *The Freedom of Self-Forgetfulness* (Lancashire: 10Publishing, 2012).

Hannah Anderson, *Made for More: An Invitation to Live In God's Image* (Chicago: Moody, 2014).

James Berg, *Changed Into His Image: God's Plan for Transforming Your Life* (Greenville: BJU Press, 1999).

David & Krista Dunham, *Table for Two: Biblical Counsel for Eating Disorders* (Greensboro: New Growth Press, 2021).

More books from the Track series:
Edward T. Welch, *A Student's Guide to Anxiety* (Fearn, Ross-shire: Christian Focus, 2020).

Sharon James, *A Student's Guide to Worldview* (Fearn, Ross-shire: Christian Focus, 2020).

Ligon Duncan and John Perritt, *A Student's Guide to Sanctification* (Fearn, Ross-shire: Christian Focus, 2020).

Jason Thacker, *A Student's Guide to Social Media* (Fearn, Ross-shire: Christian Focus, 2023).

David Ayers, *A Student's Guide to Dating, Marriage, & Sex* (Fearn, Ross-shire: Christian Focus, 2023).

Reformed Youth Ministries (RYM) exists to serve the Church in reaching and equipping youth for Christ. Passing on the faith to the next generation has been RYM's mission since it began. In 1972, three youth workers who shared a passion for biblical teaching to high school students surveyed the landscape of youth ministry conferences. What they found was a primary emphasis on fun and games, not God's Word. They launched a conference that focused on the preaching and teaching of God's Word – RYM. Over the last five decades RYM has grown from a single summer conference into three areas of ministry: conferences, training, and resources.

- **Conferences:** RYM hosts multiple summer conferences for local church groups in a variety of locations across the United States. Conferences are for either middle school or high school students and their leaders.
- **Training:** RYM launched an annual Youth Leader Training (YLT) event in 2008. YLT is

for anyone serving with youth in the local church. YLT has grown steadily through the years and is now offered in multiple locations. RYM also offers a Church Internship Program in partnering local churches, youth leader coaching and youth ministry consulting services.

- **Resources:** RYM offers a growing array of resources for leaders, parents, and students. Several Bible studies are available as free downloads (new titles regularly added). RYM hosts multiple podcasts available on numerous platforms: The Local Youth Worker, Parenting Today, and The RYM Student Podcast. To access free downloads, for podcast information, and access to many additional ministry tools visit us on the web – rym.org.

RYM is a 501(c)(3) non-profit organization. Our mission is made possible through the generous support of individuals, churches, foundations and businesses that share our mission to serve the Church in reaching and equipping youth for Christ. If you would like to partner with RYM in reaching and equipping the next generation for Christ please visit rym.org/donate.

TRACK
CHRISTIAN
LIFE

A STUDENT'S GUIDE TO
DATING,
MARRIAGE &
SEX

DAVID
AYERS
SERIES EDITED BY
JOHN PERRITT

ISBN: 978-1-5271-0966-7

Track: Dating, Marriage & Sex
A Student's Guide to Dating, Marriage & Sex
David J. Ayers

Chastity is a word that isn't used much these days, but it means exercising sexual self-control in line with the moral teachings of the Bible. It means honoring God, respecting others, and embracing the liberating beauty of God's order. But how do we do that in today's recreational dating culture? And how do we think about dating and, ultimately, marriage? David Ayers has written this helpful little book to help you think through these questions, and understand why this is such an important part of the Christian life.

Christian Focus Publications

Our mission statement —

STAYING FAITHFUL

In dependence upon God we seek to impact the world through literature faithful to His infallible Word, the Bible. Our aim is to ensure that the Lord Jesus Christ is presented as the only hope to obtain forgiveness of sin, live a useful life and look forward to heaven with Him.

Our books are published in four imprints:

CHRISTIAN FOCUS

Popular works including biographies, commentaries, basic doctrine and Christian living.

CHRISTIAN HERITAGE

Books representing some of the best material from the rich heritage of the church.

MENTOR

Books written at a level suitable for Bible College and seminary students, pastors, and other serious readers. The imprint includes commentaries, doctrinal studies, examination of current issues and church history.

CF4•K

Children's books for quality Bible teaching and for all age groups: Sunday school curriculum, puzzle and activity books; personal and family devotional titles, biographies and inspirational stories — because you are never too young to know Jesus!

Christian Focus Publications Ltd,
Geanies House, Fearn, Ross-shire,
IV20 1TW, Scotland, United Kingdom.
www.christianfocus.com
blog.christianfocus.com